Nick's father was an ) to
Australia now?' he as can
go to Australia later. for
you now. And you c here
with only eight hundred pounds, you know.

His mother and father didn't like Nick's plan. They wanted him to go to college, but he wanted to go to Australia for three months. He worked in the surf shop and he had eight hundred pounds in the bank now.

His mother and father didn't understand. He didn't want to wait – he wanted to go now, not later.

It was a hot Saturday in early July. The water and sky were blue in the afternoon sun and there were some big waves for the surfers. A lot of them were in the sea.

Nick was there, too. He sat on his surfboard and waited for a good wave. A big wave came – Nick started to swim strongly.

His board moved quickly with the wave and Nick stood up on it. He was a very good surfer.

There were some Australians on the beach. They were there for the surf...and for the big surfing competition at the beach in a week's time.

One of them was a tall girl with long dark hair – Janelle. She was from Queensland. She watched Nick and then looked at one of the boys with her.

Mike smiled. 'He's very good, and that's a strong wave. It'll be difficult to beat him in the competition.'

The second boy, Brian, was small with long hair and cold blue eyes. Janelle was his girlfriend.

'We can beat him easily,' Brian said. 'He's only good because he knows the beach here. I can surf well on any beach. I want to catch some waves.' He walked down to the sea.

'I don't want to go in the water now,' Janelle said. 'Let's go and have a drink at the café.'

Brian sat on his surfboard and watched Nick in the water. 'Mike and Janelle are wrong,' he thought. 'He's not very good. He catches some of the waves OK, but he has an old surfboard – he won't win the competition with that. I'll beat him.'

It was eight o'clock that evening. Only three or four surfers were in the water. It was time to go home. Nick put his things in his bag.

'Hi. What are you doing?' It was Janelle. 'Why are you on the beach? You're usually in the water!' she smiled.

'I know,' Nick said, 'but it's late and I'm going home.'

'Will you be in the competition on Saturday?' Janelle asked.

'I don't know,' Nick answered. 'My board is old and I can't win with it. And Brian and Mike are good.'

Janelle smiled again. 'They're good, but you're good too, you know.'

They walked back up the beach and Nick talked about his plan to go to Australia, and about his mother and father. Janelle listened quietly.

Then Nick looked at her. 'What can I do?'

'Well,' she said, 'the first prize in Saturday's competition is a thousand pounds. But you're right – you can't win it with that old surfboard. Go and talk to the people in the surf shop in town. They know you and they know your surfing. Perhaps they'll give you a board for the competition, with the shop's name on it. That's good for them and good for you. But listen: you've only got one week before the competition.'

The morning after, Nick and his mother were in the kitchen.

First Nick went to the surf shop in the town, then he went to the beach.

Nick was in the sea all that afternoon. It was a sunny day and a lot of people were in the water. The waves were good and Nick was very happy with the new board from the surf shop.

Mike and Brian were there, too. They watched him.
'It'll be difficult to beat Nick on Saturday,' Mike said. 'He's got that new board now. He knows the sea here.'
Brian didn't answer.

Later in the afternoon Janelle arrived at the beach. Brian and Mike were at the café.

Nick saw Janelle on the beach and swam in to her. He wanted to talk to her.

'Hi,' he said. 'You were right. The people in the surf shop liked the plan. Look, I've got a new board with their name on it ... only for this week and for the competition.'

'Right,' Janelle said. 'Now you can win the competition – it'll be easy.'

'Why do you want me to win?' Nick asked.

Janelle looked at him and smiled. 'Because you're good. That's why.'

Suddenly they heard a noise. There were a lot of people near the café.

Janelle and Nick ran across the beach. Near the café, Janelle stopped and asked one of the surfers, 'What is it?'

'It's your friend, Mike,' the boy answered. 'He had an accident . . . cut his foot. It's bad. He can't walk. He won't be in the competition on Saturday now; not with a bad foot.'

Brian and some other people were with Mike.

'There was some glass on the beach – I didn't see it,' Mike said.

'He's going to the doctor,' Brian said to Janelle. Then he looked at Nick.

'You can go – we don't want you here,' he said.

Nick started to answer angrily, but Janelle put her hand on his arm.

'I'm sorry about your foot, Mike,' he said.

Mike smiled. 'Thanks, Nick. I know that.'

After Mike's accident Brian didn't talk to Nick.

Mike is hurt and Brian is angry – I don't know why. He wants to win this competition.

What's wrong with Brian? What did I do?

But can I beat him?

Yes Nick. But Brian is very good and he doesn't like you very much. Did you talk to your father about Australia again?

No.

Why not?

OK, OK. I'll talk to him this evening. But he'll say no again.

Nick was right. That evening his father was not happy.

'You're asking us for money,' he said.

'Only the money for the plane to Australia, Dad. I have eight hundred pounds in the bank, and I can win the prize money from the competition this weekend – that's a thousand pounds – I'll have one thousand, eight hundred . . .'

'I don't know about this, Nick,' his father said. 'I'll talk to your mother about it.'

The day of the surfing competition was hot and sunny. In the morning all the surfers tried to catch the good waves. The judges watched from the beach. Nick and Brian surfed well all morning.

Nick did not have time to talk to Janelle in the morning but she waited for him before the afternoon competition.

'You're doing well,' she said. 'There are only four very good surfers in the competition and you're number two, after Brian. Good luck!'

In the afternoon the waves were very big but Nick was a strong swimmer and his new board was good. He sat on it in the water and waited.

A big wave arrived and Nick started to swim strongly.

Nick caught the wave well and stood up on his board. The people on the beach watched – it was exciting to see.

Suddenly Nick heard a noise.

A surfboard hit his right arm. He fell from his board. A second big wave hit him and he saw Brian's board coming at him . . .

His head went under and the water was in his mouth. His arm was hurt; he started to swim but it was not easy.

He sat on his board and moved slowly in to the beach. He was tired and it was difficult to move his right arm. When he arrived he put his board under his left arm and walked up the beach.

People looked at him. Some of them started to talk to him, but he didn't want to talk. He sat on the beach and looked at the waves.

Janelle walked across the beach to him.

Nick didn't answer. Brian walked angrily away up the beach with his surfboard.

Nick and Janelle found Mike at the beach café.

'Hi,' he said. 'Congratulations! Oh, Nick ... a man was here to see you. Where is he now?'

It was Nick's father.

'Dad! What are you doing here?'

His father smiled. 'I came to watch the competition,' he said.

'But you said "surfing is dangerous".'

'I'm right, too. Surfing *is* dangerous – that was a bad accident this afternoon on that wave. But it's very exciting, too. And Janelle and Mike are right – you're a very good surfer.'

'How do you know Janelle and Mike?'

'I met them this afternoon. They talked to me about Australia and Queensland and the surfing there. I have a question for you.'

'What is the prize for winning today's competition, did you say?' his father asked.

'A thousand pounds,' Nick answered. He was excited. 'Can I go, Dad? Can I go to Australia?'

'Well,' his father said, 'with today's prize money and your eight hundred pounds in the bank, you can live there for two or three months. OK, Nick. Your Mum and I will give you the money for the plane to Australia. But in October you'll be back here in England for college. Right?'

'Right!'

'And a second question.'

'What?' Nick asked.

'Can you win that competition in September in Australia, too?'

Nick looked at Janelle. She smiled at him and then at his father. 'It'll be difficult to stop him,' she said.

ACTIVITIES

Pages 1–13

Before you read

1 Talk about these questions. What do you think?
   a Is surfing dangerous? Is it exciting? Is it difficult?
   b What do you know about Australia?
2 Look at the Word List at the back of the book. What are the
   words in your language?

While you read

3 Are these sentences right (✓) or wrong (✗)?
   a Nick wants to go to Australia before college.   .....
   b Nick has a lot of money and an expensive
     surfboard.   .....
   c Janelle, Mike and Brian are from America.   .....
   d The first prize in the competition is a thousand
     pounds.   .....
   e The people in the surf shop give Nick a prize.   .....

After you read

4 Answer these questions.
   a Why is Nick's father angry?
   b Why does Nick want to go to Australia?
   c Where does Nick meet Janelle?
   d What do Mike and Brian say about Nick?

Pages 14–26

Before you read

5 Talk about these questions. What do you think?
   a Who will win the competition? Why?
   b Will Nick's father help him?

While you read

6 Write the right word.

    a Mike hurts his ....

    b Nick asks for money for a ticket to ....

    c Brian's surfboard hurts Nick's ....

    d The .... says, 'it wasn't an accident.'

    e Nick's .... watches the competition.

After you read

7 Why are these things important to the story?

    a surfboard   glass   Nick's father   the judge

8 Which words are right?

    a Janelle first meets Nick on the beach in the *morning/ afternoon/evening*.

    b Nick's mother thinks, 'Surfing is *bad/dangerous/ expensive*.'

    c Brian says to Nick: 'You are *good/bad/dead*.'

    d Nick's father and mother give him money for *a surfboard/ the ticket to Australia/college*.

9 Talk about these people in the story.

    Nick   Mike   Janelle   Brian   Nick's mother

Writing

10 Write about three of the people in the story.

11 First, Nick's father doesn't want to help him. Why not? But after the competition, he helps Nick. Why?

12 You are one of the judges. Write about the surfing competition.

13 You are Nick. You go to the surfing competition in Australia in September. Write a letter to your mother and father about Australia and the competition.

WORD LIST *with example sentences*

accident (n) There was a car *accident*, and the driver is dead.

arm (n) He's a good swimmer because he has strong *arms*.

beach (n) Let's sit on the *beach* and look at the sea.

beat (v) England *beat* Germany 2-1 in yesterday's game.

board (n) I can't surf well. I can stand on the *board*, but I often fall off it.

college (n) After school, he was a *college* student for three years.

competition (n) She's a very good dancer. She came first in a dance *competition*.

Dad (n) Her father came in. 'Hi *Dad*,' she said.

dangerous (adj) Don't swim here. It's *dangerous*.

hurt (v/adj) I played football yesterday and I *hurt* my foot.
I'm going to the doctor because my foot is *hurt*.

judge (n) She came first in the competition because the *judges* liked her.

will (v) *Will* she be here tomorrow? Yes, she*'ll* be here, but her friend *won't* be with her.

plan (n) I'm going to have a holiday, and then I'm going to get a job. That's my *plan*.

pound (n) How much is this hat? It's twenty *pounds*.

prize (n) She's a very good player, and she has a lot of *prizes*.

sat (v) We didn't sit on the beach; we *sat* in a cafe.

saw (v) I didn't *see* her, but I *saw* her friend.

surf (n/v) I've got a new *surf* board. I love *surfing*.

wave (n) The boat went up and down on the *waves*.

win (v) He's going to *win*! Yes! He's the *winner*!

The Adventures of Tom Sawyer
Mark Twain

Tom Sawyer loves adventures. He has them at home, at school,
and with his friends – Huck Finn, Joe Harper, and Becky Thatcher.
Tom has one adventure in a graveyard, one in an old house,
one in a cave. Who does he see in those places – and why is he
afraid?

Twenty Thousand Leagues under the Sea
Jules Verne

This is the story of Captain Nemo and his submarine, the *Nautilus*.
One day, Nemo finds three men in the sea. For months the men
live on the *Nautilus*. They find a town on the sea floor, beautiful
coasts and a lot of gold. But they want to go home. Can they
escape from Nemo's submarine?

Rip Van Winkle and The Legend of Sleepy Hollow
Washington Irving

Rip Van Winkle walks into the mountains one day and meets some
strange old men. He comes home twenty years later. One dark
night, Ichabod Crane is riding home and sees a man on a black
horse behind him. The man has no head. Are there ghosts in these
stories? What do you think?

*There are hundreds of Penguin Readers to choose from – world classics,
film adaptations, modern-day crime and adventure, short stories,
biographies, American classics, non-fiction, plays ...*

For a complete list of all Penguin Readers titles, please contact your local
Pearson Longman office or visit our website.

www.penguinreaders.com

Pearson Education Limited
Edinburgh Gate, Harlow,
Essex CM20 2JE, England
and Associated Companies throughout the world.

ISBN: 978-1-4058-6969-0

First published by Penguin Books Ltd 1996
Published by Addison Wesley Longman Ltd and Penguin Books Ltd 1998
New edition first published 1999
This edition first published 2008

5 7 9 10 8 6 4

Text copyright © Paul Harvey 1996
Illustrations copyright © Bob Harvey (Pennant Illustration Agency) 1996

The moral right of the author and of the illustrator has been asserted

Typeset by Graphicraft Ltd, Hong Kong
Set in 12/14pt Bembo
Printed in China
SWTC/04

Published by Pearson Education Ltd in association with
Penguin Books Ltd, both companies being subsidiaries of Pearson Plc